STAYING CLEAN

Living Without Drugs

STAYING CLEAN

Living Without Drugs

First published August, 1987.

Copyright © 1987, Hazelden Foundation.
All rights reserved. No portion of this publication
may be reproduced in any manner without the written
permission of the publisher.

Library of Congress Catalog Card Number: 87-80783

ISBN: 0-89486-447-5

Printed in the United States of America.

Editor's Note:
   Hazelden Educational Materials offers a variety of information on chemical dependency and related areas. Our
publications do not necessarily represent Hazelden or its
programs, nor do they officially speak for any Twelve Step
organization.

CONTENTS

1. Find New Friends................................1
2. Don't Start Using Drugs 3
3. Examine Prescription Drug Use 4
4. Avoid Alcohol 4
5. Avoid Beer and Wine............................5
6. Live Just for Today 5
7. Use the Serenity Prayer 6
8. Learn the Slogans...............................7
9. Forget Old Ideas...............................10
10. Stick With the Winners 12
11. Tend to Our Recovery, No One Else's.............13
12. Attend Nar-Anon 15
13. Make Personal Decisions in Pursuing Romance.......16
14. Beware of False Assurances......................19
15. Keep an Open Mind.............................19
16. Remember, Our Disease is Progressive 20
17. Become Active.................................22
18. Use the Telephone 24
19. Choose a Sponsor 26
20. Deal Positively With Insomnia....................30
21. Analyze Clichés...............................31
22. Confront Resentments 34
23. Beware of Self-Pity............................36
24. Enjoy Life but Beware of Overconfidence 37
25. Remember Our Last Drug High 39
26. Be Grateful 40
27. Be Good to Ourselves..........................42
28. Avoid Alcohol and Other Drug Occasions 43
29. Change Daily Habits 45
30. Go to N.A. Meetings 47
31. Beware of Excuses.............................51
32. Seek Professional Help 54
33. Work the Twelve Steps 56

INTRODUCTION

The way to recover from drug addiction is to practice the Twelve Steps of Narcotics Anonymous (N.A.). There is no easier way. However, some of us are unable to immediately accept the spiritual route as our only hope. Many of us have had to try to stay clean for awhile before we could clear our heads enough to even consider accepting the Twelve Steps.

Here are some of the ways experience has shown us how to avoid continuing or resuming our drug habits.

1 Find New Friends

What are our friends going to say if we quit taking drugs with them? What are we going to do when they bring out our favorite drugs?

We must first decide whether our life or our addicted friends are more important to us. Many have learned the hard way that hanging around using buddies may tempt us more than we can stand. If we do not change our social environment from drug-ridden to drug-free, the chances are good we will go back to using almost before we start to go clean.

Remember we are still addicted, no matter how long ago we stopped using drugs. If we follow the program outlined by Narcotics Anonymous we will recover, but the disease stays with us, requiring ongoing Step work. Something in us cries out for drugs. It is only common sense at first to stay away from places and people who make drugs available.

"Give up old friends?" the newcomer will cry. "Why they're the only people I trust. I've never trusted anyone who wouldn't use with me."

That is part of the problem. Our whole lives have been built around addicts and addiction. But we do not have to stop associating with addicts. Narcotics Anonymous is full of new people we can trust. They are just like we are . . . addicts one and all. But they are addicts who have stopped using drugs.

The addicts in N.A. understand not only our addiction but our determination to never again succumb to it. We can trust them because they have been where we have been. They are safe to be around because they have stopped what we want to stop. They are ready and willing to help us quit drugs and stay clean.

"But I can't desert my old friend," newcomers will declare. "He needs this program as much as I do."

What he or she needs is of little consequence. Narcotics Anonymous is a program for those who want it, not for all who need it. It would be a miracle if our friends wanted to stop as much as we do at exactly the same time. We must face up to the reality that our friends probably do not want to clean up their acts right now. They may never want to.

It is all we can do to take care of ourselves, especially at the beginning of our N.A. way of life. Desert our friends? We have to if they are on drugs. We must put a lot of space between ourselves and drug-using friends if we want to survive and get well.

If friendship is stronger than drugs, our friends can follow us into N.A. But they will have to do that by themselves; we cannot do it for them. We can learn right now that friendship may not be stronger than drugs. Trying to put friendship first can keep us from recovery. It can kill us.

Anyone who has a desire to stop taking drugs is eligible to join N.A. As addicts, we each must find our own way. The best we can do for friends who still use is mind our own business. First we must get well. Only then will we be able to assist anyone who asks for help; this even includes old friends if they do approach us. If that happens it will be on their timetable, not ours.

Meanwhile, we must replace our addicted friends with clean friends who we can trust. N.A. is not only a great recovery fellowship, it is an organization where we can make new friends.

2

Giving up drug-using companions to save our own lives is not as tough as it seems. We may be amazed to discover that after we are clean for awhile we have little in common with that old gang.

It is time to shed still-using friends along with our sick old ways. We will find all the new friends we need in Narcotics Anonymous as we share their recovery.

On the outside, we can find new friends among those who do not use drugs. Once we are clean, we will find all kinds of non-using new friends. We may be amazed at how sociable we become once we are off drugs. A whole world exists of wonderful people both in and out of N.A., and we are going to love them and be one of them. We will discover that people who are not using drugs are more interesting than people who are.

2 Don't Start Using Drugs

A sure way to stop taking drugs is to never start. A certain way to never get stoned is to turn down drugs. Some people say the first drug we tried was the one that got us into trouble. There can be no argument against this fact once we are clean: If we always turn down the first drug, we will never get stoned.

As addicts, we cannot use drugs in moderation. We can't start or we go all the way. The choice is ours. We can say "yes" or "no" to the first drug. If we say "yes" the drug takes over.

It is up to us. If we want to stay clean, the answer each time we are offered a drug or tempted must be "no." There is no other way to stay clean.

3 Examine Prescription Drug Use

As recovering addicts, we may ask, is it safe to take medicine prescribed by a doctor? No one but a physician is qualified to judge whether an addict or anyone else needs medications to sustain life or mental stability. It is important that our doctors understand the nature of our addiction. They must understand it is difficult to break addiction while using any kind of mood-altering substance, prescribed or not. Only physicians are qualified to determine if drugs are vital to medical treatment of diseases, but it is up to you to inform physicians of your addiction. Physicians cannot properly treat our medical problems unless they know of the dangers of prescribing mood-altering drugs to us.

If we have been using a legal prescription for a long time, such as Valium or other barbiturates, we can find a doctor who is familiar with Narcotics Anonymous. If that's not possible, find an N.A. member who is a physician, or look for someone who specializes in treating addiction. Ask if we should stop using the prescription and how we can stop using it safely. Remember, detoxifying ourselves can be dangerous, so we need help.

We can get off mood-altering drugs with the help of a doctor who has experience in treating our disease. We should do it as quickly as it's safely possible. Only this approach will help us become clean like those who recovered before us. And we don't have to jeopardize our recovery by allowing an uninformed doctor to prescribe mood-altering drugs to us.

4 Avoid Alcohol

Some of us looked down on those who drank alcohol. Alcoholics seemed less sophisticated to us than drug users. Well, here is some news for those who still think that way:

Alcohol is a drug. The surgeon general has proclaimed, "Alcohol is our nation's number one drug problem." Alcohol is just another drug and addicts can easily substitute it for our drug of choice.

We do not stay off drugs by taking drugs. The N.A. member who wants to stay clean will not drink alcohol. To be clean we must also be sober.

5 Avoid Beer and Wine

Way back in 1933 when prohibition was repealed, a law was adopted which introduced the legal sale of beer and wine on U.S. military bases. The ridiculous theory was that no one could get drunk on wine or beer.

Do not be taken in by the foolish notion that drinking beer or wine is okay as long as you do not touch the hard stuff. It is all alcohol. A one-ounce jigger of whiskey, a four-ounce glass of wine, and an eight-ounce glass of beer each contain the same amount of ethyl alcohol, one of the drugs we must avoid to stay clean.

We can't kid ourselves; drinking wine or beer is not safer than using other drugs. Those of us who turn to alcohol are invariably off and running again into addictive despair.

6 Live Just for Today

Saying no to ourselves each time we have an opportunity to use drugs for the rest of our lives may seem impossible if we look at it as a lifetime project. But in Narcotics Anonymous we have found an easier way to stay clean. All we have to do is stay away from mood-altering substances — just for today. Any of us can resist temptation for one day no matter how miserable it gets. We can take anything for a day. We don't have to worry about tomorrow. We can live and stay clean in the now, one minute at a time.

If we can keep ourselves off drugs today, we can do the same tomorrow. We need not constantly worry about tomorrow. All we need to do to stay clean for one day is to turn down drugs right now. We stay clean for a day . . . just for today.

There are a lot of friends and tools in N.A. to help us through a clean day.

7 Use the Serenity Prayer

One way recovering addicts find to stay clean through the day is through prayer. Many N.A. members use the Serenity Prayer:

God, grant me the serenity
To accept the things I cannot change,
Courage to change the things I can,
And wisdom to know the difference.

We can use this prayer daily or many times daily. This simple prayer helps addicts stay away from drugs just for today. As addicts, we pray to accept our disease that makes it impossible for us to control our use of drugs. We cannot change that. We can change and pray for the wisdom to know that using drugs again may be fatal. We can also pray for the courage to not start using again. With such wisdom and courage we can get through a day in good shape.

Miracles have resulted from the Serenity Prayer. However it is not a short cut to the spiritual awakening necessary for recovery from our disease. That comes later in the Twelve Steps.

Using the Serenity Prayer often will help us stay clean until the Twelve Steps remove all desire for drugs from our minds.

8 Learn the Slogans

Five slogans are commonly used with the Twelve Steps by addicts who never want to use again. In meeting halls around the world these slogans are often hung in this order:

Live	Easy	But	Think,	First
and	Does	for the	Think,	Things
Let	It	Grace of God . . .	Think	First
Live				

They are arranged so the first word of each slogan offers sound advice to the addict when read left to right, *Live Easy But Think First.*

Live and Let Live

If we are to have the peace of mind necessary to lick our addiction we need to learn not to let the behavior of others bother us. At the very least we must develop tolerance. Ideally our tolerance will become acceptance.

A sure way to feel miserable is to fail at something. There is nothing more doomed to failure than trying to get others to behave the way we think they ought to. Every time we base our peace of mind on the performance of someone else we are probably going to be miserable.

We can't enjoy being clean when we're miserable. If we want to be happily clean, it is better to not expect too much of other people. We had better accept it when others do things we don't think they ought to. We must let others live as they like.

Another way to be miserable is to try to behave the way we think others want us to act. No matter how hard we try, it can't be done. We cannot recreate ourselves to please other people. We fail and become miserable every time we try. This shatters the peace of mind we need to stay happily clean.

We must learn to live our lives and allow others to live theirs. When we tolerate their behavior they will better tolerate ours.

Easy Does It

As newcomers, one of the most difficult things to believe is that N.A. is an easy program to follow. How could it possibly be easy to stay off drugs?

There are only Twelve Steps to recovery in Narcotics Anonymous. They are easy to follow once we make up our minds to do so. The problem is deciding to recover.

If we have decided we want what N.A. has to offer, we are ready to take certain Steps. We are ready for these Steps when we want to stop using mood-altering substances just for today for the rest of our lives. If we are willing to go to any length to do so, the Steps become easy. If we only halfheartedly want to quit, or only want to stop using for awhile, the Steps become impossible.

The only easy way to stay clean is to practice the Twelve Steps of N.A. Until we learn how to do the Steps it is a good idea to try not to get too frantic over anything. Instead of going into a flap when things do not seem to be going our way, it is a good idea to sit down, take a deep breath, and remind ourselves to take it easy. We don't need to resolve our entire future in one day, and taking it easy helps us stay clean.

But for the Grace of God

We can remember why we are clean. Seeing someone who is not clean is a good reminder of where we have been and where we need not return if we leave our lives up to the grace of God.

Some of us continue to envy those who still use drugs, but this envy won't last for long. In N.A., we see the results of addiction in other users who are not fortunate enough to be on the road to recovery.

We will probably see the degradation and despair of one who has slipped out of the fellowship and returned to substance enslavement. It is a reminder of what can happen to us if we lag in our determination to stick with N.A.'s Twelve Steps to recovery.

"There but for the grace of God go I," we can honestly say when we learn of someone's death by overdose, or death by violence associated with addiction.

"There but for the grace of God go I." Remember it. It will help us stay off drugs just for today.

Think, Think, Think
One of the most popular slogans found in meeting rooms all over the world is

Think,
Think,
Think.

A new N.A. member struggling to recover may at any time be tempted to use a mood-altering substance. No excuse to take drugs is acceptable to the newly clean member who wants to stay that way. However, some situations make us more vulnerable to temptation than others. If such an occurrence unexpectedly occurs we can stop and think before we act rashly and put ourselves under even more pressure to return to drugs.

"Think first," is a good suggestion for those of us who are not yet trained to cope with people, places, or situations that prompted us to use drugs before.

First Things First
When we arrive in N.A. we are usually told we do not have to worry about staying clean for the rest of our lives. We only have to turn down drugs just for today. We can remember, *First Things First*. If we take care of today, tomorrow will take care of itself.

Take the First Step, then the next. Apply the same principle to everyday living. Do what comes next. Do not try to handle everything at once. Do what the slogan says: *First Things First*. This approach will help us stay free of chemicals just for today.

Live Easy But Think First

This slogan is composed of the first words of each of the other five sayings. It cautions us to take it easy and think about what we are going to do before we act.

Later on, the Twelve Steps of recovery will make it possible for us to trust our intuition. Until we take the Steps we had better watch ourselves. Do not panic. Take it easy. Think before you act. Do not use, no matter what!

9 Forget Old Ideas

It is obvious our old ideas of how to live were not healthy. They got us into states of helpless desperation, and we had to seek rescue from N.A.

We must get rid of the ideas that led us to drugs in the first place. We must dispose of all the excuses we used to justify drug use even after it began causing us nothing but pain, trouble, and humiliation.

The first idea we have to erase is the notion that anything good can come of using drugs again. We have to demolish any ideas we may still have that it is desirable to take drugs.

The most obvious idea we need to get rid of involves any lingering fantasy that we can or will be able to exert even the slightest control over any mood-altering substance.

Those are the more glaring ideas we must get rid of. It may not seem so to the struggling addict whose body has not yet had time to cleanse itself of chemicals, but those are the easiest ideas to shake. Our present predicament may have already convinced us we are powerless over addiction.

Numerous ideas may exist within us that are even trickier to let go of. These include:
- We cannot get along without our old drug-related friendships.
- People who do not use drugs can't be trusted.

- The law is our enemy.
- It is not normal behavior to say "no" to drugs.
- Life without drugs will be boring.
- The behavior of other people can drive us to drugs.
- Drugs are necessary to have good sex.
- Losing sleep is more unhealthy than withdrawal from drugs.
- Prescription drugs are okay because they are legal.
- It is okay to switch to alcohol to ease the pain of withdrawal.
- Marijuana is not as dangerous as other drugs.
- A job is too important to take time off from to deal with drug-related problems.
- We can handle our addiction by ourselves.
- There is something wrong with someone who goes to "too many meetings."
- Increasing the intake of nicotine, caffeine, and food is all we have to do to stay off drugs.
- A meeting a week will cure us.
- It is impossible to recover from addiction.
- Addicts never recover.
- Old-timers in the program have nothing to offer because they are too old and out of touch with younger people.
- God will take care of us whether we ask Him to or not.
- There is no Power greater than ourselves.
- It is as bad to become addicted to N.A. meetings as it is to be addicted to drugs.

Old ideas such as these can kill us. One old idea often heard at N.A. meetings can do us in. There is a mistaken notion that no one ever recovers from addiction. The truth is this: The disease of addiction is one we will carry with us until we die, but recovery is possible through abstinence and continuously working the Steps.

Nothing can be more discouraging or more baffling to our recovery than trying to embark on a program of recovery if we believe it is impossible to stay clean. On page 83 of the Basic

Text of *Narcotics Anonymous*, we are told, "Now we know that the time has come when that tired old lie, 'Once an addict, always an addict,' will no longer be tolerated by either society or the addict himself. We do recover."

Narcotics Anonymous is based on principles found in a book published by Alcoholics Anonymous called *Twelve Steps and Twelve Traditions*. This book was written by A.A.'s co-founder, Bill W.

Narcotics Anonymous explains on page X,

The Twelve Steps of Narcotics Anonymous, as adapted from A.A., are the basis of our recovery program. We have only broadened their perspective. We follow the same path with a single exception; our identification as addicts is all-inclusive in respect to any mood-changing, mood-altering substance. . . . We have by no means found a 'cure' for addiction. We offer only a proven plan for daily recovery.

10 Stick With the Winners

We can remember to share experience, strength, and hope with all in N.A. But when we want to know how to recover, we ask those who are recovering.

A recovering member of N.A. is one whose compulsion to use drugs has been removed by God. A recovering addict tries to practice N.A.'s Twelve Steps in all his or her affairs as suggested in Step Twelve. Those who are recovering have done so by means of the Twelve Steps of recovery and are now dedicated to carrying the message of those Steps to other addicts.

A recovering addict goes to N.A. meetings not just because he or she has to, but because he or she wants to. A recovering person no longer uses the program only for what he or she can get out of it but for what he or she can contribute to it. A recovering addict serves the fellowship in many ways; these can include being on committees, Twelve-Stepping, sponsoring newcomers, moving chairs, making coffee, and holding office.

Little is gained by sharing misery with the miserable. Look for the happy members. They will not only share their happiness, they will share how they got that way so we can be happy too.

We can help the unfortunate but heed those who succeed in N.A. The adage — "like begets like" — was never more true than in our fellowship. If we hang out only with losers, we lose. We can help them, and by so doing we will be helping ourselves. And we can let winners help us.

We can spot the winners. They radiate success. They are not just clean, they are happily clean. They are grateful for their drug addiction because without it, they might never have heard of the Twelve Step pathway to a drug-free life and a joyous way of living.

God shines through N.A.'s winners. He shines upon you. Stick with the winners and be free.

11 Tend to Our Recovery, No One Else's

Some of us may be intimately involved with someone who is addicted. We may have to decide what is more important to us — our clean life or our relationship. It is up to each of us. We should allow no one else to interfere with our decision. It is a personal matter that each of us must take full responsibility for.

Misery loves company. The addict going through withdrawal will often desperately wish his or her partner were taking that same miserable journey at exactly the same time. This is not likely to happen.

Joy loves company, too. The N.A. newcomer experiencing "cloud nine" ecstasy in the first stages of freedom from drugs will naturally want to share this new-found treasure with the one he or she loves. But the gift of being drug free can seldom be fully shared with other active drug addicts, even the one we love most in this world.

Addicts who depend on someone else's freedom from drugs to stay clean are doomed from the start. It is a life and death matter. Two addicts leaning shakily on each other cannot cut it. If one falls, they both fall. Each addict who really wants to recover has got to do it only for himself or herself.

There are plenty of recovering addicts willing to help by sharing how the Twelve Step program of recovery works for them. The using addict must not be allowed to hinder our recovery, no matter how much we love that person.

We cannot follow the Twelve Step program for the one we love. We cannot get the one we love to do it for us. In this situation, our only hope is to mind our business. And our business is what we personally do about our drug problem, not what anyone else does — especially the person closest to us.

Each of us must decide whether to leave or stay with a loved one who returns to or never stops using alcohol or other drugs. This, like our recovery, is nobody's business but ours.

The decision should be based upon only one qualification. We can each ask, "After I do what I decide, will I live a happy, drug-free life? Or will I get dragged back into the drug pit?"

If you think you can remain unaffected by your loved one's addictive behavior and not let it pull you down, proceed with great caution. You can be prepared to bail out anytime it becomes necessary.

You can also bear one policy in mind at all times: What your partner does about alcohol or other drugs is his or her business, not yours.

12 Attend Nar-Anon

Anyone trying to recover who chooses to live with or form a close attachment to a practicing addict needs to learn the art of detachment. If there is a Nar-Anon group available, join it.

If we remain with a loved one who still uses drugs, we can benefit from belonging to both N.A. and Nar-Anon. We can practice both programs at once.

If there is no Nar-Anon group available, then we need to try to detach on our own. Detaching from someone we love does not necessarily mean leaving that person. But it does mean giving up our concern with or trying to change that person's behavior, especially his or her addictive behavior.

Narcotics Anonymous is a save-your-own-life fellowship. Nar-Anon is a mind-your-own-business program. If we are living with or in love with an addict, we need both programs.

Just as N.A. is a fellowship of men and women who want to recover from drug addiction, Nar-Anon is a program for those who need to recover from living with addicts. Recovery can be achieved only by practicing the same Twelve Steps.

We can ask ourselves if we are subconsciously seeking an excuse to take drugs again. It is alluring to allow someone else's outrageous behavior to get us so upset we think we need a mood-altering substance to calm down. But an addict trying to recover can never afford to take drugs for any reason, let alone because of the way some other addict behaves.

Sooner or later someone we feel close to is going to use drugs. They do it because they are addicts. It is natural behavior for addicts to use drugs. If we think we have to use drugs because of their behavior, we are doomed. We will never recover if we use others as an excuse to use.

An addict easily upset by another addict's behavior needs Nar-Anon more than a nonaddict does. When we slip we start using again. That can kill us. Nar-Anon is available not only to teach us how to cope with friends and relatives who use drugs, but to help us recover from being "addicted" to another addict.

The secret of N.A.'s success is that addicts who are recovering can, as no one else can, help other addicts recover from the need to take drugs. But it all goes down the tube if we let active addicts drive us back to drugs.

Some addicts who have broken the drug habit cannot tear themselves away from others' addiction. But in this case, the symptom of our addiction involves trying to control someone else. Nar-Anon can help us recover from this final and just as fatal symptom of our common disease.

If another addict's actions or words bothers us at all, we need to go to Nar-Anon.

13 **Make Personal Decisions in Pursuing Romance** Depending upon our point of view, many of us are either lucky enough or unlucky enough to be drawn into a new emotional involvement during our first few months in the program. This seems to happen even though we have heard well-intentioned advice from Nar-Anon members to refrain from getting involved with anyone for at least a year.

First let us be clear about one point: Such advice is personal, based upon someone else's experience and opinion. There is no mandate published by N.A. to refrain from emotional involvment during the first year.

Ours is a program for staying away from drugs just for today. It is not a program to stay away from love or sex for a year.

There are no hard and fast rules about intimate relationships. It is a controversial issue. The Twelve Steps do not specifically address this and no N.A. publications address if or when a newcomer should become emotionally or sexually involved. Therefore, it is an outside issue.

Tradition Ten says, "Narcotics Anonymous has no opinion on outside issues. . . ." Our love life is our business, not the business of our N.A. group or sponsor.

Nevertheless it would be best to be forewarned that a newcomer entering the jousting ground of romance, whether it includes sexual activity or not, is uniquely vulnerable to the temptation to use drugs. When we gamble with the emotions of love, we may enter an arena of ecstasy, despair, or both.

In the past most of us used chemicals to help us avoid coping with the highs and lows of passion and rejection. Now we do not have drugs to fall back on.

In a program that teaches us to live just for today while not becoming too lonely, it is confusing to try to abstain from intimate involvement for an entire year. Giving up drugs is about all most of us can handle, and not many of us get through a year without emotional or sexual involvement.

The answer is obvious: We are very likely to become emotionally involved whether we want to or not. If we deny our feelings or restrict our behavior we may become frustrated and tempted to turn to drugs.

We who succumb to romance do run the risk of rejection. When we begin a relationship we take the risk of being dumped. But getting dumped is no reason to turn back to drugs. Our hearts can be broken. We may experience excruciating pain. But pain is not a motivation to resort to mind-numbing drugs. We can get so high on love, sex, or both that we think nothing can hurt us. But being involved with someone does not remove our addictions.

None of these ecstasies or calamities is acceptable as an excuse to use drugs! *We do not use drugs for any reason.* We do not use because of joy, despair, ecstasy, rejection, or heartbreak.

Do not believe it if someone warns us that emotional involvement during our first year in N.A. will cause us to take drugs. We can promise ourselves right now that with the help of the program nothing will drive us back to drugs, not even love that doesn't prove true. In N.A. we learn how to experience life and love without chemical assistance.

Be warned there are predators of both sexes in every group. Such thoughtless N.A. members will try to take sexual advantage of a newcomer. Sexual seduction is no less common in Narcotics Anonymous than any place else. Those who practice indiscriminate seduction do not care who they hurt. Personal gratification takes priority over consideration for their victims. Beware of the "thirteenth steppers" who add vulnerable newcomers to their scores. But whether we avoid being a victim or not, we do not let what happens drive us back to drugs.

In N.A. we do not use, no matter what.

Professional counseling may help us sort out our relationship and sexual problems, if necessary. Neither our N.A. group or sponsor is apt to be a reliable authority on love or sex. We will run into members with lots of experience, but they can't solve our problems. It would be no wiser to turn our love life over to the management of an amateur than to place our legal problems or physical ailments into the hands of other addicts who, like ourselves, have no legal or medical training.

Addicts who, despite all the risks involved, go ahead and become involved with someone will need all the common sense they can muster. Established couples as well as those new to romance must learn to detach from the problems of their partners. Each must take care of himself or herself.

"Stick with the winners" is even more pertinent for those seeking a mate than for those trying to establish friendships.

We can try to avoid relationships with people who are plagued with problems. We can start looking for companionship in people who have healthy approaches to living.

If a new relationship is based on previous addiction to the same drugs, it is not likely to turn into a marriage made in heaven. Furthermore, an addict falling for another addict should start attending Nar-Anon.

14 Beware of False Assurances

Whether a relationship involves friendship or romance, we can remember to be wary of forming a close attachment to anyone who refuses to believe we are addicts.

Many recovering addicts have fallen for a friend's assurance of, "You know, I don't think you are really addicted at all. I think you could enjoy getting high with me now."

As addicts, we cannot find an enemy as dangerous as a husband, wife, lover, or best friend who refuses to accept the reality of our disease. Tragic consequences can result from listening to someone who says, "Just this once won't hurt you."

If we love our lives, we can reject the assurances of anyone who keeps trying to convince us we are not really addicts. It is hard to believe one who claims to love us would deny our addiction, but it happens all the time. We have got to be ready for this kind of temptation and be ready to get away from it when it occurs.

Love does not conquer all. It does not conquer drugs. We will be better off without a lover or friend who refuses to believe we are addicts.

15 Keep an Open Mind

We can remember to keep ourselves receptive to new ideas because the Narcotics Anonymous recovery program requires a 180-degree shift in the way we think.

We don't have to blindly accept everything we hear at an N.A. meeting or everything our sponsor tells us. But we can't dismiss what we hear without thinking it over and talking it over with recovering addicts. If we do not investigate all we hear with an open mind, we might miss good advice vital to our recovery.

We don't have to make the same mistakes that addicts before us have already made. That is why we have literature. It is intended to keep us from making the same mistakes. The wrong moves of those before us have been identified the hard way. They have been analyzed for us by others who survived them.

We will sometimes hear an N.A. member say, "I don't know how this program works, but it works." How it works is clearly spelled out in the Basic Text of *Narcotics Anonymous* and the Twelve Steps. In fact, Chapter Four of *Narcotics Anonymous* is titled "How It Works."

On page 17, the Basic Text states: "The steps are our solution. They are our survival kit. They are our defense, for addiction is a deadly disease. Our steps are the principles that make our recovery possible."

Only an open mind will make way for new ideas which must replace the old if we are to recover from our fatal disease. If we really want to recover we must be willing to learn a new way of life that is totally alien to how we were taught in the past to conduct ourselves.

Preconceived notions of how to stay off drugs may keep us on them. Staying clean must now become the most important purpose in our lives. In order to do so we need new knowledge to replace what previously never worked. A closed mind will keep such information from entering our consciousness.

We will also hear some say, "Don't intellectualize. Utilize." What they really mean is, "Take action."

Earlier we discussed the slogan, *Think. Think. Think.* Keep your mind open. Use it to learn what action to take to get well.

16 Remember, Our Disease is Progressive
Drug addiction is not just a bad habit. It is a progressive, often fatal disease. We must remember that.

In the past when we were able to stay clean for awhile, we began to feel so physically well that we thought we had recovered enough to start using again.

But after we started using drugs again we quickly discovered we were not well enough to safely use again. And we found we were worse off than before. The sickest of us told ourselves we had not stopped long enough to safely indulge in our favorite drugs again. The very fact that we even wanted to use again proved we had not recovered. When we did use again we suffered even more than before.

N.A. reveals to us the true picture of our progressive disease. No length of abstinence will allow us to safely return to drug use.

Addiction is a disease we can continually recover from as long as we never again experiment with mood-altering chemicals. If we do, we quickly find ourselves in the deep despair of our disease again. Our disease gets progressively worse whether we are clean or not. Once we start again, no matter how long we have been off drugs, our illness has increased as if we had been using drugs all along.

Experience shows that when an addict of long abstinence returns to any kind of drug, he or she experiences horrifying deterioration into a helpless state as advanced as if he or she had never abstained.

Remember, we have a progressive disease. Believe it if you value your life. Do not test it. It is best to believe it and never forget this fact.

We can help ourselves abstain if we remember a relapse can kill us.

17 Become Active

Every addict who quits using drugs asks the same question, "What will I do with all my time now that I've stopped?"

One symptom of addiction is that we cannot imagine a lifetime without drugs. We only do it just for today. But many of us cannot fathom getting through even a whole day without the routine associated with using. We have an almost terminal fear of being bored.

The best way to not become bored is to get active. The first thing to do is go to a lot of meetings. If there is more than one daily meeting in your area, attend more than one daily meeting.

Those who go to five meetings a week learn five times as much about how to recover than those who go to one weekly meeting. Those who go to ten meetings a week learn twice as fast as those who take in five.

Meetings are seldom boring once we are able to listen to what is being said. Everything we hear is so new we do not initially understand much of it. But if we keep listening we begin to make great discoveries about fellow addicts and ourselves. Learning our secrets is never boring to anyone as self-centered as we are by the time we get to N.A.

At first some may not want to join group discussions. Those who do not wish to share are allowed to pass when called upon. There is no disgrace in not talking because we have nothing to say. We will often be told, "The newcomer is the most important person in the room." Such recognition is never boring to an addict who needs love and attention.

Some of us who really need stroking quickly learn a sure way to get a round of applause. All we have to do is identify ourselves by first name as an addict and tell how many days we have been clean, no matter how short the time has been. When we do so everybody claps. We hear shouts of, "All right!" Such acclamation is not boring at all.

When we get enough nerve to share at meetings we find another way to keep from getting bored. We get to hear ourselves talk. Not only that, we discover that others in the meeting room lean forward to listen to what we say. For a minute or two we may even feel like the most important person in the room. That kind of stardom is seldom boring.

Before long we will discover a person in the room who is even newer in the program than we are. We get outside ourselves for the first time and share with the newcomer how we managed to stay clean. Not long ago the only way we could get outside ourselves was to take a chemical that did not even work well any more. Helping someone who is just one hour newer to the fellowship than we are is not boring.

Then we learn if we come to the meeting early we can set up chairs, make coffee, or lay out literature. When the meeting breaks up we can put away chairs, clean ashtrays, or help the group secretary lock up. This gets us into one-on-one conversation with someone with more time in the program than we have. What other addicts have to tell us may not be what we want to hear, but it will not bore us.

Before we know it we find ourselves adjourning to a restaurant or someone's house for socializing laced with laughter and talk of N.A. recovery. Somehow our horror stories of drug use become less devastating, even funny with the passage of time. We find that clean N.A. members rarely bore us. In fact most are downright interesting. Some are exciting to be with.

New N.A. friendships are an antidote against boredom.

We may not feel like dancing without drugs yet, but someone will talk us into going to an N.A. dance. There are lots of them in most communities. Fear of dancing while clean will leave us when someone drags us onto a dance floor filled with recovering addicts who are enjoying themselves.

There are N.A. picnics and conventions to go to. N.A. motorcycle club outings, trail rides, camping weekends, retreats, birthday parties, banquets, and other social events take place so often we cannot get to them all.

We can show our gratitude to N.A. by volunteering our time. Each group has paperwork to do, supplies to purchase, meeting notices to post. Transportation to and from meetings can be provided to those who do not own cars. Newcomers can accompany old-timers on Twelfth Step calls to assist suffering addicts who call the N.A. phone number for help. Intergroups, service committees, and central offices all need your help. Engaging in N.A. volunteer work will keep us in touch with the most vital recovering members of our fellowship. They may bless us with recovery, but they will not bore us.

Get active in other ways, preferably with N.A. friends. Go to baseball, basketball, and football games. Go fishing. Attend plays, movies, and concerts. Swim, run, surf, sail, or ski. Replace the highs you used to seek in drugs with the healthy elation exercise, entertainment, and sports can provide.

We can get high on living all we want. Keeping turned on to life will help keep us turned off of drugs.

Staying clean will bring new clarity to our brain. Use it to have fun. Make it fun to be free of drugs.

18 Use the Telephone

There is not always a meeting to go to at the exact moment we feel we need one. There may be no other N.A. members present when we need their support or counsel. The telephone then can become a vital part of our recovery process.

Ask those you meet in N.A. for phone numbers. They will be glad to furnish them. They will be happy to receive calls when we need to talk to someone who has experienced the same problems we have without taking drugs.

We aren't calling someone to talk us out of using drugs. The purpose is to learn how to not want to use — even in periods of stress.

It is much easier to stay clean if we have someone to talk to who knows what we are going through because he or she has already survived the same or a similar experience.

It is an even better idea to phone other members when there is no immediate problem. It is a way to keep in touch, to keep N.A. principles handy in our defense arsenal. Remember when we call any N.A. member we are also helping that person experience the loving bond that exists between those dedicated to staying off drugs and becoming healthy human beings.

Do not take it as a personal affront if someone we call happens to be too busy at the moment to talk. The other person might be in the midst of an important activity and cannot be interrupted. We can accept that the first person was busy and call someone else.

We must never depend exclusively on one person, not even when making an emergency phone call. We can pick up the phone again and call someone else in the fellowship. That is why we need a lot of phone numbers.

Usually the member we call will be delighted to hear from us. We may have to learn to allow enough time to talk so we do not have to cut off the person before he or she feels like ending the conversation.

We all know meetings help us stay clean. In some areas there are many meetings or there may be only a few with hours or days between them. But calling another member on the phone can become a meeting between meetings.

A Narcotics Anonymous meeting is defined as "whenever or wherever two or more N.A. members gather together." Fortunately, when there are no scheduled gatherings N.A. members can get together on the telephone.

We do not have to feel embarrassed to call late at night when we feel we need help. Ours is a disease of isolation. We must do something to get over our deliberate loneliness. We can always phone someone.

We can get extremely lonely when we're wide awake and worrying in the wee hours. We need support no matter what time it is. We will get it. N.A. members care about each other 24 hours a day.

Ten to one, when we end the conversation the person we have awakened will thank us for calling. With new friends only a phone call away, who needs to feel lonely?

The telephone is a godsend to addicts who want to recover. It can be used to ask where meetings are, to seek advice and support, to call for help, or to spontaneously give encouragement to someone who can use it.

Many of us have found it helps to call a few members every day whether we need to or not. It is a way to develop friends and have fun. It is one of many ways N.A. gives us to begin having such good times we would not think of lousing it up with drugs.

"Make someone happy," was once the jingle of a telephone company commercial on television. We can remember this and call someone in the program. Make another N.A. member happy. It will make us happy too.

19 Choose a Sponsor

Before we have been in Narcotics Anonymous very long we will begin to spot certain members who have the kind of recovery we want. We discover we can trust such people with secrets about ourselves that we would not admit to others. We may decide to ask such a person to be our sponsor.

N.A. members often say that choosing a good sponsor can make a big difference between recovering and not recovering.

The primary purpose of a sponsor is to help us understand the Twelve Steps to recovery well enough to practice them in all our affairs. A recovering addict who agrees to sponsor us will try to guide us from Step One through Step Twelve. A good sponsor will try to answer our questions about the Steps and advise us how to practice them.

Before selecting a sponsor it is helpful to know what a sponsor can be expected to do for us. It is also helpful to recognize what he or she is not qualified to do.

A sponsor should help us take each of the following Steps. These Twelve Steps are the only program of recovery offered by Narcotics Anonymous.

1. We admitted we were powerless over addiction, that our lives had become unmanageable.
2. We came to believe that a Power greater than ourselves could restore us to sanity.
3. We made a decision to turn our will and our lives over to the care of God *as we understood Him.*
4. We made a searching and fearless moral inventory of ourselves.
5. We admitted to God, to ourselves and to another human being the exact nature of our wrongs.
6. We were entirely ready to have God remove all these defects of character.
7. We humbly asked Him to remove our shortcomings.
8. We made a list of all persons we had harmed and became willing to make amends to them all.
9. We made direct amends to such people wherever possible, except when to do so would injure them or others.
10. We continued to take personal inventory and when we were wrong promptly admitted it.
11. We sought through prayer and meditation to improve our conscious contact with God *as we understood Him,* praying only for knowledge of His will for us and the power to carry that out.
12. Having had a spiritual awakening as the result of these steps, we tried to carry this message to addicts, and to practice these principles in all our affairs.

These Twelve Steps are our entire program of recovery. How our sponsors help us understand and follow these simple yet difficult suggestions is between them and us. We can be sure to pick a sponsor who we think knows a lot about these Steps.

The friend we trust to guide us in the Steps should suggest we go to a lot of N.A. meetings, but he or she should also let us decide which meetings we attend.

An N.A. tradition states that "the primary purpose of an N.A. group is to carry the message to the addict who still suffers." The message refers to the Twelve Steps. Step Twelve says, "Having had a spiritual awakening as the result of these steps, we tried to carry this message to addicts. . . ."

We can't expect a sponsor to do our program for us. We must learn to do that for ourselves. In selecting a sponsor, we can't seek someone who we hope will nag us into going to meetings, reading the literature, or taking the Steps. Just look for someone who is trustworthy to answer our questions about the program. We can find a sponsor who is willing to share experience so we will not have to make the same mistakes he or she made.

Look for a sponsor who will provide information rather than management. Try not to choose one who is still struggling with recovery. We want to learn how to get well, not stay ill with a sponsor who is not recovering.

It is a sign of continued illness if a sponsor tries to manage our personal affairs. The purpose of a sponsor is to assist us in applying N.A.'s Twelve Steps to our lives, not tell us how to manage our unmanageable problems. Beware the sponsor who says, "I admit my life is unmanageable," while trying to manage our problems.

A sponsor is not a lawyer, theologian, psychologist, financial planner, or sex therapist. An N.A. sponsor is usually an amateur in these fields with plenty of personal failures to prove it. Is it logical to expect a sponsor who cannot manage his or her life to manage ours?

Most of all, a sponsor should be our friend. Pick someone who we want to be our friend and has recovered by practicing all Twelve Steps.

A good way to test a potential sponsor is to seek advice about a personal matter. If the prospect precisely details how to handle a problem, pass that person by. Look for a sponsor who will show us how to apply N.A.'s Twelve Steps to the problem. The Twelve Steps are the only solution N.A. offers to any difficulty.

When we find the person we would like to be our sponsor, we just ask. If that person says yes, we have a sponsor. If the response is no, we keep looking.

Any recovering N.A. member ought to be willing to help another member. It does not require much time or energy to answer questions about how to work the Twelve Steps if the sponsor refrains from meddling in personal affairs.

We have lost nothing if the person we ask already sponsors too many to take on another. A sponsor who minds his or her own business sticks to advising about the Steps. Such a person can sponsor many people. One who meddles too much into the personal lives of those he or she sponsors will have time to "manage" only a few. The first is the kind of sponsor to look for.

Changing sponsors should not be a big deal either. We need not "fire" one sponsor to adopt another. There is no requirement to mention it. We can just start asking someone else who we feel is more qualified to answer our questions.

There is no law against having more than one sponsor. We can have as many as we like.

We need not even inform the person we choose that he or she is our sponsor. Too formal a sponsorship might tempt another all-too-human addict to try to manage our life.

All we need is someone who we can confide in, someone qualified to tell us how to apply the program to life's problems instead of using drugs, someone who is an example of how to get well.

We should not look for a father, mother, brother, sister, manager, nagger, or boss. Above all we do not wish to become dependent upon even one other human being. N.A. and our sponsor should teach us to depend only upon our Higher Power.

Beware of the sponsor who fires those who do not obey orders. Recovering sponsors humbly serve those who want to get well. They neither give orders nor fire anybody.

When we choose a sponsor, we can start by defining what we want. We can ask our choice to help us practice the Twelve Steps of Narcotics Anonymous. That is the proper role of a sponsor.

20 Deal Positively With Insomnia

Most of us have a terrible time trying to sleep at night when coming off drugs. The first thing to remember is that it is not dangerous to lie awake at night. No one dies from lack of sleep.

Trying to fall asleep never works. It is not something we accomplish by trying. In fact, trying to make ourselves go to sleep actually keeps us awake.

Instead of frantically attempting to go to sleep, we can take our time and experiment another way. We can decide not to care whether we fall asleep or not. Some find not caring whether we drop off or not can cause us to doze off.

Make use of the quiet while awake in the night. Use it to practice the First Step. Just as we admitted our powerlessness over addiction, we can look at our insomnia in the same way. Let our Higher Power handle both.

Music may help still our racing brains. Reading is also an old standby for insomniacs in and out of N.A. Pick up a book and read it. Read *Narcotics Anonymous* and learn more about recovery.

Newcomers to N.A. sometimes panic when they are unable to fall asleep in the middle of the night. We must resist the cunning, baffling, and powerful insanity that it would be better to take a chemical to help us fall asleep.

It is not often in this noisy, fast-paced world that we can enjoy solitude. It helps us through a long night to thank God for the rare opportunity sleeplessness offers us to cherish peace and quiet seldom available by day.

We can wrap darkness around us like a lover's arms. Listen to tiny sounds in the dark. Try to figure out what they are. Make a game of the night.

Usually when we give up trying to go to sleep and let our Higher Power have His way we wake up all too soon to find it is morning. We wonder what happened to the still of the night we were only beginning to enjoy when we fell asleep.

In the evenings that follow, we can try again to use quiet darkness for something better than sleep. This time use the wee hours of peace and silence to meditate. Thank God for such rare moments of tranquility.

Solitude is a gift. Let us cherish it the few times it comes our way, especially at night.

21 Analyze Clichés

In addition to the slogans there are many clichés repeated over and over again in Narcotics Anonymous. These bromides are no substitute for working the Twelve Step program of recovery. However there are truths to be learned from most of them, and falsehoods to beware of in some of them.

Perhaps the most common of these is KISS, which stands for *Keep It Simple, Stupid.* The first three words are good advice. The humorous salutation of the fourth word is misleading. *Stupid* is used only in jest. No one intends to imply that those of us who quite naturally complicate most things in our lives, including our own recovery, are stupid. We are human, not stupid.

Keeping it simple means sticking to the Twelve Steps. Do what they say without interpreting them. The Steps are explicitly written and mean word for word exactly what they say.

Keep it Simple means do not complicate any Step to make it say what we think it ought to mean. It means, do not revise a single Step.

Adhere precisely to the suggestions made in each Step, one through twelve, to recover from drug addiction. It means, follow the simple order of the Steps.

Later when we have recovered through practicing all Twelve Steps we will learn to pick which Steps to selectively apply to problems as they arise. But the newcomer is advised to *Keep It Simple.*

Do the Steps in order the first time around. This will keep us busy enough for some time to come. Nobody can do all Twelve Steps overnight.

If we get frantic trying to juggle these unfamiliar Steps or from illogically skipping back and forth among them, we become vulnerable. Anxiety, even over the Steps, is an unhealthy state of mind for a newly clean addict.

Serenity should gradually increase as we move logically from the First Step, where we recognize our disease, to the Twelfth Step, where we carry what we've learned to other addicts.

Do not be afraid to ask for help from a sponsor or another recovering N.A. member who appears to be calm. Heed advice which seems uncomplicated. Usually that advice should be to turn our life over to our Higher Power's care. We can give our Higher Power full charge of our will and then trust it. Get used to one method of confronting problems. Always turn to the Steps and those who can help work them.

Meanwhile stay as calm as possible. The simpler our thinking becomes the more sanely we behave. Keeping it simple at least gives us momentary serenity.

Instead of *Keep It Simple, Stupid,* KISS should stand for, *Keep It Simple and Serene.*

Another cliché which can be helpful or harmful, depending on how it is applied, is *HALT.* HALT stands for Hungry, Angry, Lonely, and Tired.

When we become too hungry, too angry, too lonely, too tired, or any combination of these states we become more vulnerable than when we are well-fed, calm, in good company, and well-rested. But our program must be something other than trying to totally avoid being hungry, angry, lonely, or tired. One of the first things we admit to in this program is that our lives are not manageable by us or anyone else except our Higher Power.

Hunger, anger, loneliness, and being tired should simply put us on guard. At such vulnerable times we turn to our sponsor, meetings, literature, and the Steps to see us safely through.

Obviously we try not to unnecessarily become too hungry, angry, lonely, or tired. But when we find ourselves in a state which once would have moved us to seek solace in drugs, we now seek sustenance from N.A. friends, literature, and the Steps.

When we find ourselves excessively hungry, angry, lonely, or tired, *HALT!* We can stop what we are doing or feeling for awhile. Turn to the program. Get help from Narcotics Anonymous.

That is what the program is all about.

One of the most useful clichés heard around the world is *Stay Out of Slippery Places.*

No matter how determined we think we are to not use drugs again, it makes no sense to hang out in places where others go to get stoned. Nothing can be gained from returning to the scene of the crime, but much can be lost. We can lose both our minds and our lives.

Old habits are hard to break. Socializing with the old gang we used drugs with may put more temptation directly under our noses than we can stand. Not only are the examples of those around us bad, but the availability of our favorite or other drugs may be more than we can handle.

Some people believe we who insist on frequenting drug users' environments are not putting enough room between our new chance for life and our old disastrous way of existing.

What is there in an old haunt for a recovering addict who wants to be clean? Are we still so fascinated with the life-style that brought us groveling on our knees for help that we cannot do without it? The main attraction of that scene was the drugs, and we claim to want to stay free of that. What would we want to go back to our old haunts for other than the drugs? The people? Those who hang out in such places are stoned. Do we want to join them?

Let us not kid ourselves. Wanting to hang around others who are still using is a sure sign we too want to use again. We must stay out of slippery places if we do not want to relapse.

There are a lot more clichés. Analyze them. Look for the good and the bad in them. Use only the good. And remember that the most useful clichés are only temporary tools to help us stay clean long enough to work our full Twelve Step program of recovery.

22 Confront Resentments

Resentment is the most dangerous time bomb addicts confront. We have already discussed the unlikelihood of always being able to avoid anger. Resentment is hanging onto anger, and it can kill us.

Resentment does nothing to the person or persons we resent. It has no effect on them. It only affects us. It makes us miserable. Resentment is not only sustained anger, it is perpetual misery — misery preserved indefinitely.

Resentment has been used more than any other emotion as an excuse to return to drugs. Justifiable resentment has been especially used. Justifiable resentment is when someone else has done something so awful to us that we think we are justified in feeling miserable.

Feeling miserable long enough can make us feel righteous about seeking revenge. For an addict this often means getting stoned again just to get back at the person who hurt us. But the only one who gets hurt is the addict.

Getting stoned *at* someone we resent makes as little sense as punching ourselves to get even with another person. Yet we do it. We nurture our resentments with a passion equaled only by our subconscious desire to return to drugs at any excuse.

Nothing is easier to find than injustice done to us by someone else, even by someone we love. "I'll show that so-and-so," we cry as we reach for the drug. "This is her fault, not mine!"

Many an addict has blamed his or her return to addiction on a lover or spouse. But it was not the lover who did the greatest wrong. The addict did it to himself or herself with drugs.

34

Justifiable resentments that we nurse and preserve all too often lead to irrational behavior. For an addict, that can mean using drugs. What else could calm us down from anything as complex as "irrational rationalization" of irrational behavior? If we want to survive as clean addicts, we must do something about our resentments as soon as they start to build. We can get rid of them by a quicker and safer way than by drifting off to doomsday on a cloud of deadly drugs. There has to be a better way to handle resentments than to use drugs.

There are several ways.

We can close our eyes, visualize the person we resent and envelope that person in light. It is not easy to continue resenting someone we see bathed in our own light.

We can pray for the one we resent. It is very difficult to resent and pray for someone at the same time.

Sometimes our resentments are so deep rooted we find it almost impossible to bathe the source of our misery in light or to pray for the person we so vividly hate. What then are we to do?

We can apply a little reason to our resentment. We can remember the other person may be as sick as we are or were. That person's action or lack of action we feel so justified in resenting may be only a symptom of his or her illness. Instead of resenting that other sick person, we could feel sorry for the one we resent. It is hard to resent a person we feel sorry for.

It is also difficult to feel sorry for someone we really resent. There is a sure way to get rid of a resentment: we can forgive the person we resent. That should do it. Forgive that other person. Then we can forgive ourselves. The resentment will be gone.

And remember, even a justifiable resentment is not acceptable as an excuse to use drugs.

23 Beware of Self-Pity

Too much concentration on ourselves is not a good way to comfortably stay clean. The worst kind of self-obsession is when we feel sorry for ourselves.

Self-pity can be the most pervasive of all emotions. Thinking about how bad things are going for us completely blocks out any view of how well things might be going. One little discomforting experience can so wrap us up in our misery that we will be unable to recognize opportunities for joy and success.

"Poor me. Woe is me!" Self-commiserations to that effect are often the last words of an addict before returning to the all enveloping, futile indulgence of trying to smother our troubles with drugs. We become totally absorbed with ourselves when things do not go our way. Our only thought of our Higher Power is to blame Him for letting whatever bothers us happen to us.

We feel betrayed by people and by our Higher Power. Beware of such exaggerated concern over how badly we allow ourselves to feel over matters beyond our control. Temporary disillusionment with God can tempt us to permanently turn back to the only other Higher Power we have ever trusted in a crisis. In the throes of shameless self-pity we might fire God and employ drugs.

Accept the bad as what normally accompanies the good. Winston Churchill described life as a chain made up of links of pain joined together by links of pleasure. What is to be gained from driving ourselves deeper into depression by ceaselessly bellyaching to ourselves about our misfortunes? Let us remember the lows we experience are always followed by highs.

Another cliché, *Live in the Present*, is good advice when things are going well. But when the world comes tumbling down it is better to forget about living in the now and adopt another cliché, *This Too Shall Pass*.

Remember, every low is followed by a high unless we feel so sorry for ourselves we do not allow it to happen.

Get Off the Pity Pot is another cliché we can apply to ourselves when feeling low. Or we can use the golden rule: Do unto others what you would have them do unto you.

We can get out of our misery by helping someone else. There are plenty of miserable people to help in N.A. Some of them are just coming off drugs. Others, like ourselves, have forgotten the real misery that made us ask for help in the first place.

We could be out there using again. Nothing that happens to us when we're clean can be as bad as what can happen if we return to taking drugs.

When feeling low, the first thing to do is contact another N.A. member or go to a meeting. If that is not possible, start reading recovery literature. Or pray. Ask God's forgiveness for blaming our problems on Him.

Going to others in the program in times of despair will expose us to N.A. options for handling problems. We also will learn we are not alone. Whatever is bothering us enough to make us sink to feeling sorry for ourselves has happened repeatedly to others in the fellowship. Ask how they got over it. Do what they did and we will get over it too.

No matter what, self-pity is not a valid reason for taking drugs.

---

24 Enjoy Life but Beware of Overconfidence

We can become almost as vulnerable from feeling too high as when we feel too low. Feeling overly elated can make us overconfident. Overconfidence may make us careless about working our program. Getting cocky can poise us precariously over the deep end of temptation to use again.

The unexpectedly marvelous feeling of being clean for awhile has misled many an inexperienced N.A. member to think he or she has been cured enough to use drugs again. That should not be surprising. We always felt overconfident after we had temporarily refrained from getting loaded for awhile. It always felt good.

"I feel good enough to use again," we used to tell ourselves when we had temporarily recovered from a bout of drugs that had dragged us so low we had to lay off for a time. The difference is that now in N.A. we know we never really get over it.

We must believe we can never again successfully use any form of mood-altering substance. Does that mean we should avoid getting high without drugs? Certainly not. We should take advantage of every opportunity to achieve drug-free highs. There are plenty of things to make us feel good without drugs.

Good food, music, books, nature, sex, friends, sports, movies, the theater, dances, and travel are a few ways. Marriage, job promotion, or business success can do it for us. It makes no sense to avoid living life to the fullest just because we aren't using drugs.

No matter how good we feel, we are still addicts. The use of drugs to celebrate makes us feel as high as a kite but we will always sink into the three-D depths of disaster, despair, and depression. It is not much of a fall from heaven to hell. Most of us have already seen addicted friends add the fourth dimension of using again. Why court death with drugs as the price for getting too high on life when we can stay clean?

Just remember one thing. When we feel high without drugs, that is as high as we need to get. Drugs will not take us any higher. Drugs will shoot us down.

When miraculous things happen to our clean life, enjoy them to the hilt. Feeling too good would be a ridiculous reason to gamble with drugs. Quitting is what made us feel good. We can stay clean while we are ahead.

25 Remember Our Last Drug High

We can't forget what happened the last time we used drugs. Addicts tend to remember only what was good about using drugs. When we dream about the past we skip over the last miserable experience we had with using drugs. We go clear back to a time when the drugs worked for us and made us feel good. Who would not go back to using if it would be the way it once was when drugs did what we wanted?

Well, it does not work that way. For an addict there is no going back to the good old days. Even those of us who managed to stop before we hit absolute bottom will never be able to return to where we once enjoyed getting high on drugs.

We can remember how low we got the last time. Addiction is a progressive disease. Our favorite substance will knock us even lower if we try it again. It will be as if we had never stopped at all, so remember how bad it got instead of how good it once was. Imagine how it will be when it gets even worse. There is no turning back. When it comes to drugs, we cannot go home again. It is all over for us in the drug using department. If we try it again it could very well be all over for us in every department.

Staying clean is not a lottery. We do not get lots of chances. There may be only one chance. Once clean, we have won. All we need do to hang onto our winnings is *stay* clean.

Do not fall victim to the *yets*. In comparing our history with others' take care not to assume we can safely return to using because we have not sunk as miserably low as others in the fellowship. We can't tell ourself, "I haven't been busted. I haven't turned to dealing or stealing to support my habit. I haven't been treated at a hospital for overdose, been divorced, or been disowned my family. I haven't lost my job or ended up in an institution, so maybe I'm not really an addict."

If we return to using drugs, we could very well find ourselves busted, fired from our jobs, or facing a variety of other negative consequences, including death.

Most of all, we can keep a clear picture in our clean minds about how wretched it was the last time we got stoned. Remember the fear, despair, demoralization, and physical problems we experienced the last time we got high.

If we cannot remember how awful it was, we can take a good look at a shattered disbeliever who decided to try it again. We can see how this person took the last chance and appears to be hopelessly addicted.

For those of us who keep trying to use again, the *yets* will come true. All the bad things may not have happened to us yet, but they will if we forget why we had to stop using.

Remembering our misery in the past helps us stay clean in the now.

26 Be Grateful

An N.A. member who is grateful for being clean is not apt to use again. Being ungrateful for our recovery means we have not recovered at all.

What did we have before we got here? We had a life full of problems with only the temporary solution of using drugs. What do we have now? We still have a life filled with problems. But now we have twelve remarkable ways to get through our difficulties. We have a solution to problems more effective and lasting than drugs. We have Twelve Steps to help us survive our problems.

The predicaments of living are just as real for a recovering addict as they are for the practicing addict. In fact, they are more real. As clean people, pain hurts us more now than it did while we were using drugs. Only now we accept pain and get through it with the knowledge that we are going to feel great on the other side. We should be grateful for that.

Practicing the Twelve Steps is not a way to avoid catastrophies and annoyances of everyday living. The Steps only help us to survive misfortunes and discomforts of life. They help us come out smiling. Is that not something to be thankful about?

If we feel sorry for ourselves because we cannot use drugs anymore, we are ungrateful. How can we thank a God we feel has played a dirty trick on us by depriving us of our favorite drugs?

Gratitude is a state of grace. Either we are grateful or we are not. If not, can we *make* ourselves feel thankful? We can if we stop to count our blessings.

We can think again about how we were when drugs betrayed us and how we are now. Do not look back upon the good times that preceded the bad. We can only recall the worst of our drug-using days.

Gratitude can be developed by counting the good things in our lives instead of the bad. Five percent of our experiences can make us feel awful if we ignore the 95 percent of what makes us feel good.

Shrug off the small part of living that seems to go wrong. Thank God for the healthy portion of life that goes right.

Ask why so many recovering N.A. members are grateful they are addicts. They will tell us they are grateful because if they had not been addicted to drugs they might never have gotten into N.A. Without N.A. they might never have heard of the Twelve Steps. They might have continued to disbelieve in a Higher Power or their fellow humans. They could have died thinking life consisted only of getting stoned and taking more drugs to try to avoid withdrawal.

"Thank God I'm an addict!" the recovering N.A. member will exclaim. "If I weren't I might never have gotten to this program and learned how to live."

There is much more to Narcotics Anonymous than getting off drugs. N.A. teaches us how to live life to the fullest while we are clean and to enjoy the wonder of reality.

Thank God for new friends, the great mission of carrying the message of the Twelve Steps to other addicts, and helping resurrect them to a happy life. These are things to be grateful for.

41

Some old-timers use two one-word prayers at the beginning and end of each day. When they wake up in the morning they look up to God and say, "Please." When they are ready to go to sleep at night they look up again and say, "Thanks."

It is impossible to use while thanking our God and our fellow N.A. members for keeping us clean.

27 Be Good to Ourselves

One of the best ways to avoid drugs is to keep happy and be good to ourselves.

At first some of us entering N.A. are suspicious of those members who appear to be having a good time while they are clean. All that hugging and laughing at meetings, shouting and laughter at N.A. dances, and slapping one another on the back does not seem right to us.

"This is a life and death business," some will correctly tell us, adding with a dash of discouragement, "You had better take the program seriously or you may die."

It is serious business, but that does not mean it is against the rules to have fun. We can enjoy ourselves while adhering to the Twelve Steps of recovery. In fact, they will help us enjoy ourselves more.

Some of us used drugs to have fun. Now we can learn to have fun without them. We are doing something about our problem. We deserve to reward ourselves for trying to straighten out our lives.

We have earned the right to eat good food, take long walks, enjoy good books, go to the movies, and generally have a good time. We do not need anyone else to give us these things. We can give them to ourselves. We deserve them.

Enjoying the pleasure all around us will help keep us from wanting to use again.

We do not have to go overboard in seeking these joys. Enjoying good food does not mean becoming compulsive overeaters. Being well-fed will help keep that old gnawing for drugs away as long as we do not overdo it. There is nothing to be gained from exchanging one self-destructive compulsion for another. Being good to ourselves includes taking care of our health.

Exercise is a way to be good to ourselves. We can get our bodies back in shape in order to better enjoy them. There are lots of fun ways to work out. Exercise releases tensions that may tempt us back to using.

Camping, fishing, going to art galleries, shopping, and dating are all activities to make ourselves happy. Hobbies are good replacements for drugs. Sailing, snorkeling, scuba diving, and surfing are healthy ways to have fun.

The important thing is to have fun. If we enjoy ourselves enough while we're clean, we won't dream of lousing it up by returning to our old habits. We can give ourselves a break.

There is a big, wide wonderful world out there. Staying clean makes it ours to enjoy. Go for it!

28 Avoid Alcohol and Other Drug Occasions

To safely get high on life without alcohol or other drugs we have to stop associating fun with substance-oriented occasions. We must become aware that parties which routinely include alcohol or other drugs have little to offer beyond temptation to get stoned.

If we keep going where we always went we will continue to find what we always found. We can hardly avoid misery if we keep looking in places we always found it.

It is vital that a newcomer in N.A. learn to say no. It may be too late to say no to drugs if we continually put ourselves in tempting positions. It is easier to say no when we do not deliberately place ourselves in the way of temptation.

It makes no sense to go swimming if we do not want to get wet. A swim is hard to resist when someone says, "Come on in."

In most cases, when we're invited to a party where alcohol or other drugs will be served all we have to say is, "No thank you." It is that simple. It may not be easy at first, but it is simple. If we want to stay out of harm's way we can politely turn down the invitation.

Some people may insist on knowing why we do not wish to attend social events where alcohol or other drugs will be used. It's all right to say, "Because I am trying to lay off drugs right now. It will be easier if I don't go to parties for awhile."

If our host asks why we are trying to stay off drugs, we can casually say, "For reasons of health," which is true, or "I want to quit while I'm still champ," which is humorous. Or we can say, "I have to be somewhere else," which is absolutely true if we want to stay clean.

Sometimes business or family functions obligate us to attend despite the fact that alcohol or other drugs will be served. For such a command performance, do just that. Appear and leave.

Mandatory attendance at a party will not tempt us if we remember we are there out of obligation and not to use alcohol or other drugs. A required social function will not return us to using drugs unless we decide to use it as an excuse.

Clean addicts are like subjects of hypnosis. Nothing can make us do anything we do not want to do. We do not use drugs only because we are at a party. We use them because we want to. Unless we are required to be at such a party, we may attend the party because we subconsciously want to use again more than we want to stay clean.

If we attend a party only because something other than drugs requires us to be there we will be prepared not to relapse. We will either be disinterested in drugs or prepared to resist them. To remain in that safe frame of mind is a good reason to discretely leave the party as soon as possible.

Common sense tells us the less we expose ourselves to drug-using situations, the less chance there is of using such an occasion as an excuse to drop out of N.A.

If we still find ourselves uncertain about whether or not to expose ourselves to the dangers of a social function where we know alcohol and other drugs will be served, we can ask our sponsor or another recovering N.A. member for counsel. Or ask our Higher Power.

If a situation suddenly arises when there are no N.A. members to consult, we can summon all the common sense we possess. To stay away from drugs, we can avoid places where they are easy to get. We can get away from the fire unless we want to get burned.

29 Change Daily Habits

Using drugs was a habit. Acquiring drugs was a habit. The time we made for obtaining and ingesting drugs had become routine. Our entire pattern of living had been built around specific ways and means of obtaining and using the substances we had become dependent upon. What we did while we weren't using drugs had also become part of our scheme for getting around to using drugs.

For most of us, life had become a clanking chain made up of links of getting stoned and links of feverish activity to support our habit. Now that the drug is gone, only the links of feverish activity remain.

An addict recently off mood-altering substances is likely to retain the panic that formerly kept him or her supplied. At first we are apt to head for all the same places and do all the same things we did between bouts with drugs. If we allow ourselves to follow the same chain of activity even though the drug links are missing we are liable to miss the drugs even more.

Since our lives now depend on staying off drugs — instead of frantically maneuvering to obtain and use them — we must behave each day in a new way. Our routine must change. We must learn to do things differently than we did before.

"All we are asked to do is change our course 180 degrees," many have commented in describing the new way of life necessary to stay clean.

Many clean newcomers have found it helps to vary everything they do from the way they functioned while supporting their habit. This might begin by getting up at a different time, praying for help to get through the day, or meditating.

For those of us who do not have jobs, we can start looking for one. For those of us who used to make a living in the drug trade, we must get out of it now. The notion that getting clean in N.A. might make you more efficient and prosperous as a drug dealer is too far off the beam to even discuss. Many have had to get rid of notions like that in order to recover.

Those of us who are used to hanging out on the street must find somewhere indoors to mingle with clean N.A. members. N.A. meetings are wonderful places to meet people and learn how to recover by means of the Twelve Steps.

Physical exercise can replace the time we used to devote to drug-related activities. Often we arrive in N.A. with lagging physical strength. Running, walking, pumping iron, aerobic exercising, and other ways to get back in shape offer variety from our old routines for getting through the day.

We can start taking a more active role in community and worldly awareness. We can start watching the news on television and reading a newspaper everyday. We may even want to get involved at a local level as a volunteer stuffing envelopes or ringing doorbells for a candidate or cause.

If we find more time on our hands than we know what to do with, we can try getting more education. Go back to school part-time or full-time. It is never too late to learn how to become a fashion designer or an airline pilot. There is no end of opportunities to improve a clean mind. There is no limit to the knowledge we can absorb.

Varying daily behavior can eliminate many of those common instances when we used to think of drugs. For awhile, our drug reflexes may be triggered every time we return to behavior even remotely similar to that which surrounded our past drug usage. Change the situation and we can prevent that reflex.

We can alter our daily ways. If we create new clean habits to replace the old we can give ourselves a different perspective on life. We will be amazed at how much brighter everything looks when we get out of the behavioral rut that drugs kept us in.

The easiest way to resist drugs until the Twelve Steps take over is to ignore them. Keeping drugs out of sight will help keep drugs out of mind.

30 Go to N.A. Meetings

One habit to form immediately is to go to a lot of N.A. meetings. When we wonder how often to go, consider how often we used drugs.

Many old-timers in N.A. advise newcomers to, "Go to 90 meetings in 90 days."

When a newcomer asks, "How long do I have to go to meetings every day?" the answer is, "You have to keep going until you want to go every day."

Another way of putting it is, "Go to daily meetings until you learn to pronounce *anonymity*. Continue to go until you no longer can say it."

Going to one meeting each week takes about 52 hours and $52 a year of our time and money, provided we drop a buck into the basket each time. That is not much of an investment to save our lives.

Mathematical logic will conclude that a person who goes to meetings two times a week will learn twice as much in the same time as the member who goes to one meeting a week. Those of us who go to five weekly meetings gain five times as much knowledge as those who go once a week.

N.A. members who go to meetings every day will tell us it becomes a compulsion to attend. No day seems quite complete without a meeting. How many meetings we go to is entirely up to us. It depends on how soon we want to be happy without drugs.

There is a tradition which states, "Each group has but one primary purpose — to carry the message to the addict who still suffers." N.A.'s Twelve Steps to recovery make up the message referred to in this tradition. To recover we must hear the Steps read aloud and discussed again and again until we gradually take them all.

The fewer meetings we go to the more we hurt. The worse our pain gets the more frequently we need to hear the message of the Twelve Steps. Staying away from meetings is a good way not to hear N.A.'s message very often.

Only our Higher Power can permanently relieve us of drug dependency. Frequent contact with our Higher Power is our only hope.

None of us is individually capable of maintaining constant contact with that Power greater than ourselves. No matter how hard we try to work the Twelve Steps that put Him in charge we constantly try to take back control of our uncontrollable lives.

Every time we take charge we need to find God again as quickly as possible. The easiest place to contact our Higher Power is at an N.A. meeting.

There is a saying that, "The only one who never misses an N.A. meeting is God."

Narcotics Anonymous meetings are like links in a chain. No one is always in contact with God. Yet at any moment of an N.A. meeting, someone else is in contact with the Higher Power. When we join those in contact, the rest of us can latch on.

It is impossible to leave an N.A. meeting without having experienced some sort of contact with a Power greater than ourselves. That Power will keep us clean until the next meeting if we let it.

The more we go to meetings the better chance our Higher Power can help us. Staying away from meetings only keeps us apart from God. No one willing to go to any lengths to stay clean will deliberately dodge the only Higher Power that can save us.

Just as the primary purpose of an N.A. group is to carry the Twelve Step message, the single most important reason for newcomers to attend meetings is to continually hear that message.

There are other fringe benefits obtainable when we get together to share experience, strength, and hope with N.A. members. First among these is fellowship. It is remarkably reassuring to know we are in a room filled with other clean addicts who have experienced what we have. It is nice to know we can talk about fears and uncertainties of facing life without drugs and be understood by others who have felt or are feeling the same emotions.

Most of us have always wanted to belong to something. Peer pressure from a gang or social group we wanted to belong to probably got us started on drugs. We joined those we sought to identify with by using what they were using. And when we did we dropped even further out of humanity's embrace than we had already been.

Drug addiction is a disease of isolation. No matter how many using friends we tried to surround ourselves with we were always alone. We will never be as solitary as in the misery of our betrayal by drugs. When we arrive at N.A.'s doorstep we are lonely.

No society of men and women is more united and loving than N.A. Fellow sufferers who have grown sick and tired of being sick and tired gather together in laughing, caring groups all over the world. At last we belong to something as big as the earth.

Another N.A. tradition is that, "The only requirement for membership is a desire to stop using." That simple requirement includes everyone who suffers from drug addiction, yet only those who have "a desire to stop using" can belong.

For those of us who have been feeling sorry for ourselves because we suffer our disease, forget it. If we have been crying, "Why me?" relax. Why not me? There is nothing unusual about being addicted. It is commonplace. There are addicts at all social levels from Park Avenue penthouses to cell blocks of every penitentiary on the planet. Anyone can be an addict.

If we want to be special, we can be addicts who do not use drugs. That is truly special. Only those of us who are special can become members in the fellowship of N.A. We have really arrived when we become a member of N.A. At last we belong to a fellowship of exceptional men and women who love us.

In addition to being the most successful drug recovery program in history, N.A. membership includes a vast variety of people. Members can travel to nearly any country on earth and be on a first name basis with loving friends. These N.A. meetings can help us establish friendships and find out information when we find ouselves away from home.

The principles of group therapy are at work in an N.A. meeting. While such a gathering may not be the wisest forum to air all our personal problems, it is a great place to discuss our problems with someone who we feel we can trust. Sharing experience, strength, and hope with other members at a meeting will make us feel better no matter how fouled up the day may have seemed before the meeting. For an addict with a heachache a meeting is a good substitute for aspirin. More aches and pains enter any N.A. meeting than leave it.

Newcomers may at first be frightened by all the hugging that goes on at N.A. meetings. But the value of N.A. hugging becomes appreciated. It even becomes addictive. Being hooked on hugging is far safer than being strung out on drugs.

One trait nearly all clean addicts share is extreme sensitivity. When not dulled by chemicals our brains really take stock of what goes on around us. The straight world is as full of hypocrisy as the world of addicts. Our newly cleared heads do not miss a false beat.

Hypocrisy is acutely painful to a recovering addict. We need someplace to escape the pitiful deceptions and intrigues of the real world. There is no better place to find refuge from hypocrisy than an N.A. meeting. There is no safer space than in a room full of honestly caring N.A. members.

"I need a meeting," is a feeling often shared by N.A. members. "I really needed an N.A. meeting today," is stated by participants at every meeting of Narcotics Anonymous. A sure way to stay off drugs is to, "Go to lots of meetings and don't use in between."

31 Beware of Excuses

Those who decide to leave the fellowship and use drugs again have no difficulty finding a plausible sounding reason for doing so.

"My lover left me. I can't stand the pain," is a common excuse used to take drugs. Descent to using can easily be blamed on catastrophes of love.

"I lost my job and got depressed. My doctor prescribed a mood elevator," is an often heard double excuse. The return to drugs is often blamed on employers and doctors.

"My mother died. I simply can't go to the funeral without something to calm me down," is a logical sounding cop-out.

"I got too hungry, angry, lonely, and tired, so I used again," is a four-barreled rationalization for returning to drugs.

"I had a toothache so I took a pain pill," is another way of passing the blame for popping pills.

"Everybody else was doing it," explains another addict who relapsed. "I figured it wouldn't hurt to join them just once." Using drugs can always be blamed on making ourselves socially acceptable.

"Being clean bored me to death," another rationalizes. "I need something to lift me up."

Many N.A. members who relapse use drugs after getting upset at a meeting. "That speaker was full of baloney," is the flimsy excuse. "He drove me back to drugs."

"When I called my sponsor he wasn't home," is a weak way to shift blame for using drugs again.

Even N.A.'s Twelve Steps of recovery are sometimes used to justify returning to addiction. "My Fourth Step inventory was too scary," an addict who relapsed will say. "I had to smoke a joint to face up to the truth."

Most excuses sound fragile unless we unconsciously contemplate using them ourselves. In N.A. no excuse is acceptable for going back to drugs. We can always create an excuse to use a drug. We can avoid using by avoiding fantasies which could justify drug use.

Usually the excuse is created long before we realize we intend to use it. In the cunning recesses of an addict's brain a voice whispers, "It would be forgivable to take drugs again if my child got run over by a truck."

Or that easily recognizable voice might say, "If nuclear war begins and everyone I love or know goes up in a mushroom cloud, who could blame me for using?"

Or we may create a really complicated scenario. "If I got pinned by one leg under a burning car on the freeway and the ambulance driver offered to give me a pain killer before amputating my leg, would I let him?"

Or it could be a glamorous fantasy like, "If I were sitting in a parked car in front of an apartment house and a gorgeous redhead came out to invite me in for a line of coke, would I go?"

Nothing is far fetched for the tricky mind of an addict seeking an excuse to use drugs again. Let us analyze the desperation inherent in the wild examples created to demonstrate how cunning, baffling, and powerful our disease really is.

We must be careful of what we imagine. Anything we dream might really happen. If we look closely at our favorite fantasies, we may discover intentions of returning to drug use. We may discover we're looking for excuses to return to our former drug habits.

There are two ways to handle excuses. One is to avoid them. The other is to face up to them. Recognize them for what they are.

In N.A. we hear all excuses. We collect them. We spot those used by addicts lucky enough after relapse to get back into our fellowship's welcoming fold. We identify excuses being developed by those who are about to disappear from our midst. We learn to identify excuses, so we can recognize them when we are tempted to use them.

Addicts about to leap back into the drug abyss often begin by finding fault with something or someone in the fellowship. They stop going to meetings because the room is too smoky. They do not like the secretary. There are too many sick newcomers present. They cannot stand listening to all those boring "drug-alogues."

There are those who think they cannot associate with "losers and street people" who go to N.A. meetings. The fact is the real losers are those looking for a way to excuse themselves from the group.

The reverse may also be true. Sometimes "liberals" refuse to associate with conservative "highbrows" in a group. Or we may quit because a group conscience vote is taken which goes against our concept of how meetings should be run. We can always find something in any meeting to get mad enough about to stomp out and seek surroundings conducive to using drugs again.

Boycotting a meeting because a majority of its members differ from us socially, politically, racially, or religiously is a handy way to blame the fellowship for turning us back down the endless tunnel of addiction.

Another way for an addict who wants out is to tell him- or herself there is too much "God talk" at N.A. meetings. "I didn't come here to get religion," the agnostic or atheist about to leave will complain. Refusal to recognize that N.A. is spiritual rather than religious will open a crack for a nonbeliever to fall through; this is a hell where addicts will have no power to turn their will and life over to a Higher Power.

For a member of Narcotics Anonymous there is no acceptable excuse for using drugs again.

If we find someone's reasons for using drugs again as valid, beware. If we think we would return to drugs if we had someone's problems, beware. We could be setting ourselves up to use again when similar things occur in our lives. Excuses we accept for others may eventually be employed by ourselves.

We may think accepting another's reasons for relapsing is a form of understanding. In reality, validating any rationalization for relapsing is how we store excuses to justify our return to drugs.

Collect addicts' reasons for leaving N.A. Label them clearly so we can identify them. Label them *excuses*.

No excuse for trying to escape problems by taking drugs is acceptable to us anymore. The escape route for a using addict leads to hell.

32 Seek Professional Help

At first some of us think knocking off drugs will solve all our problems. Not so. If our car breaks down we still need a mechanic. Legal problems may require us to retain a lawyer. Poor health may cause us to consult a physician.

No amount of clean time is sufficient qualification for anyone in N.A. to become our psychiatrist, financial planner, or marriage counselor. No sound business person goes to an amateur for advice on how to run a company. There are qualified business consultants for that. N.A. meetings or sponsors are not skilled in such matters.

If we need a loan we should go to a bank, savings and loan, or finance company. A professional counselor can offer better solutions to a relationship problem than any untrained person at an N.A. meeting. Specific advice on how to solve personal problems is not N.A.'s purpose.

Many of us arrive in N.A. with special needs not able to be met at meetings. There is no such thing as a legal group in N.A. to help with litigation problems. N.A. has no relationship groups to solve emotional entanglements. There are no sex groups to help with dysfunction. We do not have mental health groups to deal with psychiatric problems.

For these and many other difficulties N.A. members are no different than anyone else. We must consult professionals.

Some members will incorrectly state that those who regularly attend N.A. meetings need not consult psychotherapists. Those of us untrained in psychotherapy have no right to say such a thing under the guise of Twelve Stepping. At best, such uninformed opinion is practicing medicine or psychology without a license. At worst, it is none of our business.

N.A. does not profess to cure all ills or solve all problems. The Twelve Steps of recovery from drug addiction are the only solution N.A. can offer to help solve personal difficulties. God may motivate a troubled member to go to a psychiatrist or clergyman. Who are we to determine which of us consult family counselors or psychologists?

Only amateurs offer free advice on how to solve intimate problems. Some amateurs unconsciously try to control us by telling us precisely how to manage our personal affairs if we want to stay clean. If we feel intimidated to behave only in a certain suggested manner we may be under such a spell laid on by an amateur.

A woman who hates men will advise other women to have nothing to do with men. A man who dislikes lawyers will recommend that we defend ourselves in court. A man who abuses women will tell other men to, "Love 'em and leave 'em." A divorced person will often counsel a married person to, "Pack up and leave!"

Many professionals belong to Narcotics Anonymous. There are doctors, lawyers, bankers, and priests. A psychiatrist who belongs to N.A. would no more give free psychiatric treatment than a lawyer would handle a case in court without compensation. An N.A. member who sells cars would not provide us with a free automobile, nor would a dentist who belongs to our fellowship fix our teeth for nothing. Ask them. They will quote a price or fee for professional service. But they will charge us nothing to tell us all they know about the Twelve Steps of N.A.

Many have found it helpful to augment their N.A. program of recovery by consulting professionals to treat their addiction. There is nothing wrong with that. Most professionals who treat addiction apply N.A.'s Twelve Steps to their therapy. Nearly every reputable treatment center suggests discharged patients continue going to Narcotics Anonymous as long as they live.

N.A. in no way competes with hospitals or treatment centers. N.A. does not endorse them. They endorse N.A. Our fellowship fully cooperates with professionals who treat addiction. Our policy toward such therapists and private or public institutions is called, "cooperation with the professional community."

If any of us feel we need professional help on any matter including addiction, we should find it. Narcotics Anonymous will provide love, understanding, support, and the Twelve Steps of recovery whether we consult professionals or not.

33 Work the Twelve Steps

There is only one program of recovery from addiction; it is called the Twelve Steps. The purpose of the other techniques described in this booklet is to keep us fit to practice the Twelve Steps.

The Steps can be studied thoroughly in N.A. literature. No amount of study will be excessive. There cannot be too much knowledge of these twelve priceless principles.

They are called Steps so we will take them one at a time. They are numbered one through twelve in the order we take them.

After we have completed Step One, where we admit our disease, through Step Twelve, where we recover, we will learn to use the Steps selectively to meet specific situations. Until then we do the Steps in the following order:

1. We admitted that we were powerless over our addiction, that our lives had become unmanageable.

We acknowledge it is impossible to exert any control over drugs, including alcohol and prescriptions. We accept it is hopeless to try to manage any part of our lives, including staying clean. We cannot do it. It is useless to try. We admit it and move on.

2. We came to believe that a Power greater than ourselves could restore us to sanity.

We must believe beyond doubt that we are insane whether we are using drugs or not. This Step must apply to us in order to take it. To recover we must take all Twelve Steps. Trying to manage unmanageable lives is insanity. Trying to control what cannot be controlled is nuts. Persistently trying to manage our lives proves we are crazy. If we cannot manage anything, who can? Only a Power greater than ourselves. We need not believe this Power will restore our sanity, we need only believe such a power "could restore us to sanity." If we think it *might*, we move on.

3. We made a decision to turn our will and our lives over to the care of God as we understood Him.

We decide to do it, not to postpone it. Without delay we gamble everything we ever will be on a great unknown that might not be there. We do not ask. We do. We place 100 percent of the management of our lives into God's hands. We give up all control. He alone becomes responsible for every feeling, thought, and act. We surrender unconditionally. In answer to, "Who is going to run my life? I? Or God?" We consciously contact our Higher Power and say, "God, take charge!" No longer responsible for managing our lives, we move on.

4. We made a searching and fearless moral inventory of ourselves.

We examine our behavior. We write an inventory, not a history. What is good about us after we put God in charge? What is bad? Are we greedy or generous? Cruel or kind? Brutal or gentle? Possessive or tolerant? Dishonest or trustworthy? Manipulative or permissive? Resentful or forgiving? Insecure or confident? Guilty or innocent? Narrow-minded or accepting? Domineering or modest? Arrogant or humble? Jealous or trusting? Fearful or courageous? If fear is present it is not a fearless inventory. Repeat Step Three. Let God stock our inventory. With Him in charge there is nothing to fear.

Are we violent or peaceful? Distressed or serene? Angry or at ease? Hateful or loving? Self-pitying or grateful? Gloomy or cheerful? Pessimistic or optimistic? Reckless or careful? Disdaining or caring? Trouble-making or considerate? Sneaky or straightforward? Selfish or generous? Close minded or willing to learn? Stubborn or ready to change? Do we smoke, overeat, drink too much coffee, try to control ourselves or others, overwork, overspend, or cling to other alternate addictions?

Put it all down. Search for every symptom of illness. It is diagnosis, not therapy. That comes later. After we jot down every symptom of how ill we are today, we move on.

5. We admitted to God, to ourselves and to another human being the exact nature of our wrongs.

What is behind the defective behavior noted in Step Four? Now we analyze those symptoms. Why do we lie? Why do we steal? Why are we jealous? Is it because we do not believe God will protect us unless we manage to conceal the truth? Are we afraid God will not provide enough unless we manage to steal? Do we believe God will let someone else have what belongs to us unless we manage to hang on to it? We think we turned our lives over to God. Does our behavior indicate we still try to manage our affairs better than God can? Does the exact nature of our problems involve our lack of trust in God?

Are we angry at what someone does or at God for letting it happen? Are we agitated because we do not believe God will solve our problems? Is grasping control away from God the exact nature behind our wrong behavior?

We look behind every defect. We admit directly to God what we find. We admit it to ourselves and another person. That individual can be a friend, stranger, sponsor, therapist, clergyman, or spouse. We tell God we do not trust Him enough. We tell ourselves we trust ourselves too much. We admit this exact nature of our wrongs to another human being. We do not seek advice about this behavior. We simply admit to these three entities what is really wrong. Having deeply diagnosed and acknowledged the nature of our disease, we move on.

6. *We were entirely ready to have God remove all these defects of character.*

In the two previous Steps we listed exactly what we believe are our defects. Either we are ready to have them removed by God, or we are not. If we still want to work on our defects, we are not ready for Step Six. How do we get ready? By going back over Steps One through Five until we are ready. If we think we can manage to remove even one defect on our own, we need to go back to Step Three and admit we are powerless to do so. If we do not believe God can remove them, we need to go back to Step Two until we think He might. We have not recently taken Step Three if we are not ready to have Him do what He wants with our defects. If we are not yet convinced nothing less than removal of these defects will make us happy, we better stay with Steps Four and Five until it becomes obvious. If we want to hang on to one defective trait we better go over Steps One through Five until all resistance vanishes.

Being entirely ready to have God remove all these defects without our help is a state of grace. It comes only when we acquire sufficient humility to step out of the way and let Him do the work. When we are fully prepared to have our entire personality changed as only God can change it, we move on.

7. We humbly asked Him to remove our shortcomings.

We consciously contact the Power greater than ourselves. We do not ask God to help us remove our own shortcomings. This is not a self-improvement program. It is a program where we let God improve us. We do not specify what defects we want removed. We listed all we could. Now we allow our Higher Power to take away or leave what He wishes. Some traits we listed as assets will be removed because they are really defects. Some characteristics we thought were defects will remain because they are strengths instead of weaknesses. We let God determine our good and bad points. We do not dispute how He changes us. We must be humble enough to let Him recreate us. We accept what we become.

The true test of humility is whether we let God do what we ask Him to or not. With no strings attached we ask our Higher Power to remove our shortcomings. We then leave them alone and move on.

8. We made a list of all persons we had harmed and became willing to make amends to them all.

Unlike our Step Four inventory of what is in stock now, Step Eight is a review of our personal histories. We search our past. We list all former acts that hurt other people. We include when our failure to act hurt others. We do not put ourselves at the head of the list. This may be the first time we have ever placed welfare of others ahead of our own. We write down every instance we can remember when we deliberately or unintentionally injured someone else. We list all harm done to others whether they deserved it or not.

We keep listing the dirt we did to others until we regret it and want to make it up to them. When we are willing to make total restitution and correct whatever damage we have done, we move on.

9. *We made direct amends to such people wherever possible, except when to do so would injure them or others.*

A direct amend is more than an apology. We confront those we harmed and make restitution for the damage we did. We replace what we stole. We repay what we owe. We take blame for misdeeds we allowed others to be blamed for. We settle unpaid bills. We compensate with love, deeds, or money to those we mistreated. We expect neither gratitude nor forgiveness in return. We take whatever action necessary to set things straight. We spend whatever money it takes to make things right. Where we were guilty of abuse, we now lavish love.

If trying to correct past damage will cause further damage to anyone other than ourselves we let the matter drop. We cannot heal those we hurt by reopening old wounds or inflicting new ones. We make no restitution which will result in punishment for accomplices. We make no confession that reveals another person's guilt. We do not include ourselves among the others we must not harm.

When we have corrected every possible rotten thing that harmed someone else, we move on.

10. *We continued to take personal inventory and when we were wrong promptly admitted it.*

The inventory we took in Step Four and admitting the exact nature of our wrongs in Step Five were so important that we are now going to continue to look at our strengths and weaknesses. We will do this one day at a time for the rest of our lives. The word *continued* means two things: we are never going to be finished taking inventories and we will never be through finding wrongs for God to remove.

Having learned what to do in our written Step Four inventories and our shared Step Five analysis of the exact nature of our wrongs, we now make daily use of these techniques of self-diagnosis.

It will not always be convenient to write down our continuing inventories. We may need to take them faster than that to handle life's daily problems. In any emergency we can ask ourselves, why am I angry? Why do I worry? Why am I envious? We can answer, I am angry because I don't like the way God is running my life. I worry because I don't expect God to handle things correctly. I envy someone else because I don't trust God to give me what I need. The answer is always the same: I don't trust God. I am agitated because I grabbed control back from my Higher Power. I think I can handle things better myself. Then all we have to do is renegotiate the Step Three contract we have broken. Put God back in charge. We may return to Step Seven and ask Him to remove this shortcoming of firing God to take charge ourselves.

We start a daily habit of recognizing and admitting when we usurp God's job of running our lives. Then we move on.

11. We sought through prayer and meditation to improve our conscious contact with God as we understood Him, *praying only for knowledge of His will for us and the power to carry that out.*

In three previous Steps we have established conscious contact with our Higher Power. In Step Three we turned our will and our lives over to Him. We could not do that without making contact. In Step Five we admitted to God what we had learned was the nature of our wrongs. We had to contact Him to do that. Step Seven had us ask Him to remove our shortcomings. When we asked we made contact. Now we improve the conscious contact we already have with God.

We petition God. That is prayer. We listen to God. That is meditation. The purpose of meditation is to help ourselves empty our minds of personal concerns so the Higher Power may enter. There are many techniques to do this. Practice one of them.

Step Eleven teaches a new way to pray. In our old way of praying we ask God to fill specific needs. This Step suggests we no longer do that. It proposes praying only for knowledge of His will for us and the power to carry that out.

Praying that only God's concerns enter our brains blocks our personal wishes. Asking only for knowledge of His will for us and the power to carry that out empties our brains so the Higher Power may enter. We do not always have to use some other form of meditation. Praying only for God's will and the power to carry it out is meditation.

We spiritually awaken in this Step when we realize we never again have to spell out what we want God to do. We awaken spiritually secure in the knowledge that we need never pray for more than knowledge of His will for us and the power to carry that out. Committed to praying only that way for the rest of our lives, we move on.

12. Having had a spiritual awakening as a result of these Steps, we tried to carry this message to addicts, and to practice these principles in all our affairs.

Step Twelve confirms we had a spiritual awakening only because we took all eleven previous Steps. Now we carry this Twelve Step message to other addicts. To do so we continue to attend N.A. meetings. We apply Twelve Step principles to every aspect of living. By means of the Twelve Steps we let God manage us in everything we do rather than trying to control things ourselves.

Narcotics Anonymous offers only one path to recovery. We recover only if we practice the Twelve Steps. We do not recover unless we take and continue to work them. Those who follow the Steps recover; those who do not follow the Steps continue to suffer.

Our disease of addiction remains incurable even after we recover. All we need to do to destroy our recovery is use drugs again. Only the Twelve Steps will keep our addiction in remission. Once recovered, we need never again suffer any symptom of it. All we need to do to stay well is continue to go to N.A. meetings and practice the Twelve Steps.

Only those who are still sick believe recovery means they can safely use again. This is not so. Recovery means we no longer need drugs, nor have any desire to use them. Our compulsion is lifted.

We will also recover if we dedicate our lives, just for today, to working the Twelve Steps of Narcotics Anonymous. Learn how. Read N.A. literature. Get a sponsor. Go to lots of meetings. Do not use drugs in between meetings.

Be one of many thousands of happy addicts who have recovered through Narcotics Anonymous.

The Beginning

THE TWELVE STEPS OF ALCOHOLICS ANONYMOUS

The Twelve Steps of Narcotics Anonymous, discussed in this booklet, are adapted from the Twelve Steps of Alcoholics Anonymous.*

1. We admitted we were powerless over alcohol — that our lives had become unmanageable.
2. Came to believe that a Power greater than ourselves could restore us to sanity.
3. Made a decision to turn our will and our lives over to the care of God *as we understood Him.*
4. Made a searching and fearless moral inventory of ourselves.
5. Admitted to God, to ourselves, and to another human being the exact nature of our wrongs.
6. Were entirely ready to have God remove all these defects of character.
7. Humbly asked Him to remove our shortcomings.
8. Made a list of all persons we had harmed, and became willing to make amends to them all.
9. Made direct amends to such people wherever possible, except when to do so would injure them or others.
10. Continued to take personal inventory and when we were wrong promptly admitted it.
11. Sought through prayer and meditation to improve our conscious contact with God *as we understood Him,* praying only for knowledge of His will for us and the power to carry that out.
12. Having had a spiritual awakening as the result of these Steps, we tried to carry this message to alcoholics, and to practice these principles in all our affairs.

---

*The Twelve Steps are taken from *Alcoholics Anonymous*, published by A.A. World Services, New York, NY, pp. 59-60. Reprinted with permission.

Other titles that will interest you. . .

Day by Day

"God help me to stay clean and sober today!" That's the affirmation that closes each of the daily meditations in *Day by Day*. Recovering addicts across the country have adopted *Day by Day* as their daily meditation book because its inspirational messages augment and reinforce the N.A. recovery program. Each meditation contains thoughts and ideas about coping with today's problems while staying chemically free. And each meditation includes suggestions and space to pencil in a goal for the day, so that we can truly act upon the wisdom of each reading every day of the year. Over 800,000 recovering people use this book to maintain recovery. (365 pp.)
Order No. 1010

Needing Cocaine

Stories of Recovering Cocaine Addicts
  by Terry Webster
  A fascinating collection of personal stories from recovering cocaine addicts. Their stories tell how anyone can become a victim of cocaine addiction and how anyone can be helped through N.A. and other self-help groups. A unique and stirring look into the human experience of cocaine addiction. (56 pp.)
Order No. 1097

Relapse and the Addict

  by Richard Dunn, D.Min.
  Based upon the experiences of 202 relapsed addicts, this new pamphlet identifies eight predictable stages of relapse. The author draws insights from the N.A. basic text to outline ten major relapse triggers and ten suggestions for what to do when relapse threatens. (24 pp.)
Order No. 5410

For price and order information, please call one of our Customer Service Representatives.

Hazelden ®
Educational Materials

Pleasant Valley Road
Box 176
Center City, MN 55012-0176

(800) 328-9000
(Toll Free. U.S. Only)
(800) 257-0070
(Toll Free. MN Only)
(612) 257-4010
(Alaska and Outside U.S.)